"中国民间武术经典"丛书
Chinese Folk Wushu Classic Series

太极拳进阶教程之
24式太极拳呼吸配合法

BREATHING METHOD OF 24 FORM TAIJI QUAN

丛书主编　毛景广
Chief Editor Mao Jingguang

编　著　毛景广
Compiler Mao Jingguang

译　著　张学谦
Translator Zhang Xueqian

海燕出版社
PETREL PUBLISHING HOUSE

河南电子音像出版社
HENAN ELECTRONIC & AUDIOVISUAL PRESS

图书在版编目(CIP)数据

24式太极拳呼吸配合法：汉英对照 / 毛景广著；张学谦
译.—郑州：海燕出版社，2007.9
（中国民间武术经典 / 毛景广主编）
ISBN 978-7-5350-3556-1

Ⅰ.2…　Ⅱ.①毛…②张…　Ⅲ.太极拳－汉、英 Ⅳ.
G852.11

中国版本图书馆CIP数据核字（2007）第134484号

24式太极拳呼吸配合法
BREATHING METHOD OF 24 FORM TAIJI QUAN

出版发行：海燕出版社　河南电子音像出版社
Publish: Petrel Publishing House　Henan Electronic & Audiovisual Press
地址：河南省郑州市经五路66号
Add: No.66 Jingwu Road of Zhengzhou, Henan Province, China
邮编：450002
Pc: 450002
电话：+86-371-65720922
Tel: +86-371-65720922
传真：+86-371-65731756
Fax: +86-371-65731756

印刷：河南地质彩色印刷厂
开本：850×1168　1/16
印张：6
字数：58千字
印数：1 001-2 000册
版次：2008年12月郑州第2版
印次：2008年12月第2次印刷
书号：ISBN 978-7-5350-3556-1
定价：28.00元

"中国民间武术经典"丛书
Chinese Folk Wushu Classic Series

前 言
Foreword

　　百集"中国民间武术经典"光盘在国内外发行之后，引起巨大的反响，深受广大武术界同行的好评，特别是海外广大武术爱好者慕名而来，拜师求学者络绎不绝，并都希望看到与之相配套的文字教材。应广大读者的要求，我们以中英文对照形式编写了这套"中国民间武术经典"丛书，以帮助广大武术爱好者学习和了解博大精深的中华武术文化。

　　中华武术源远流长。本套丛书详细介绍了少林、太极、峨嵋、武当、形意等诸多门派，包括内家和外家，近300余种拳法和武功绝活儿，是目前我国向国内外推介的最权威、最系统、最全面的武术文化精品。

　　"中国民间武术经典"丛书采用图文教材与影视教材相结合的立体教学手段，全方位地展现中华武术文化精髓。每个套路邀请代表当今最高水平的全国武术冠军、正宗流派传人以及著名武术专家进行技术演练和教学示范，保证学习者获取原汁原味的技法。

　　在丛书编写过程中，得到中国武术协会副主席王玉龙先生的关照支持，我们表示衷心感谢！参加本丛书校对工作的人员有张青川、邵佳、王浩、邵倩、韩晓宁等，在此一并致谢！

The 100 sets of *Chinese Folk Wushu Classic* compact disc has received great attention home and abroad since its publication. Most foreign Wushu lovers hope to get the written teaching materials attached to it. We have prepared this series of *Chinese Folk Wushu Classic* to help them understand the Chinese martial art and Chinese culture.

Chinese Wushu has a long history which is profound in content. This series have details on Shaolin, Taiji, Emei, etc. Including internal school and external school, nearly 300 species of the fist position and military accomplishments. They are the most authoritative, systemic and comprehensive of Wushu essence.

Chinese Folk Wushu Classic Series use graphic and video materials to demonstrate the best of the Chinese Wushu. For each routine, we invited the national Wushu champions, the orthodox heirs and famous Wushu experts who represent the highest level to conduct the technical trainings and the teaching demonstrations to guarantee the original techniques of these routines for the learners.

We express our heartfelt gratitude to Wang Yulong, vice-chairman of Chinese Wushu Association for his support and help in the process of compiling these books. We also thank Zhang Qingchuan, Shao Jia, Wang Hao, Shao Qian, Han Xiaoning for their careful work in revising our books. Thanks a lot!

编者

Editor

二〇〇七年七月大暑

July 2007 Summer

"中国民间武术经典"丛书

Chinese Folk Wushu Classic Series

编写委员会 **Writing Committee**

主 任 Director

高明星 （河南电子音像出版社社长、编审）

Gao Mingxing, Proprietor, Copy Editor of Henan Electronic &

Audiovisual Press

副主任 Assistant Director

李　惠 （河南省体育局武术运动管理中心副主任）

Li Hui, Assistant Director of Wushu Center of Henan Province Physical

Education Office

杨东军 （河南电子音像出版社总编辑、编审）

Yang Dongjun, Chief Editor, Copy Editor of Henan Electronic &

Audiovisual Press

段嫩芝 （河南电子音像出版社编审）

Duan Nenzhi, Copy Editor of Henan Electronic & Audiovisual Press

毛景广 （郑州大学体育系副教授）

Mao Jingguang, Associate Professor of Department of Physical

Education of Zhengzhou University

委 员 Commissioner

马　雷 （公安部中国前卫搏击协会秘书长）

Ma Lei, Secretary-general of Chinese Advance Guard

Defy Association of Ministry of Public Security

李素玲 （江南大学体育学院副教授）

Li Suling, Associate Professor of Institute of Physical Education

of Jiangnan University

郭笑丹 （河南龙腾多媒体技术制作有限公司经理）

Guo Xiaodan, General Manager of Henan Dragon Television
Production Company

吴必强 （重庆大学体育学院副教授）

Wu Biqiang, Associate Professor of Institute of Physical Education
of Chongqing University

涂虎波 （郑州大学体育系教授）

Xu Hubo, Professor of Department of Physical Education
of Zhengzhou University

总策划 Chief Producer

高明星 Gao Mingxing

责任编辑 Editors in Charge

郭笑丹　　　赵　建　　贾大伟

Guo Xiaodan　　Zhao Jian　　Jia Dawei

"中国民间武术经典" 丛书
Chinese Folk Wushu Classic Series
作者名单 Author List

主 编　Chief Editor

毛景广　　Mao Jingguang

副主编　Assistant Editor

李素玲　　　　郭笑丹　　　　吴necessary强

Li Suling　　Guo Xiaodan　　Wu Biqiang

编 委　Members of the Editorial Board（以姓氏笔画为序 Name of a Sequence of Strokes）

马 雷	毛景宇	代小平	丛亚贤	纪秋云
Ma Lei	Mao Jingyu	Dai Xiaoping	Cong Yaxian	Ji Qiuyun
刘海科	乔 燎	任天麟	何义凡	杨 华
Liu Haike	Qiao Biao	Ren Tianlin	He Yifan	Yang Hua
杨玉峰	张亚东	张学谦	张希珍	赵艳霞
Yang Yufeng	Zhang Yadong	Zhang Xueqian	Zhang Xizhen	Zhao Yanxia
高秀明	袁剑龙			
Gao Xiuming	Yuan Jianlong			

视频示范　Video Performer

毛景广	陈小星	陈 炳	侯 雯	任天麟
Mao Jingguang	Chen Xiaoxing	Chen Bing	Hou Wen	Ren Tianlin

图片示范　Picture Illustrators

毛景广	侯 雯	张 一	段佳洁	任天麟
Mao Jingguang	Hou Wen	Zhang Yi	Duan Jiajie	Ren Tianlin

摄 影　Photographers

贾大伟	林伟峰
Jia Dawei	Lin Weifeng

目 录

EXERCISE GENERAL
KNOWLEDGE OF TAIJI QUAN

第一节

太极拳的由来与流派
THE ORIGINS AND SCHOOLS OF TAIJI QUAN

第二节

练习太极拳对身体各部位的要求
THE REQUIREMENTS TO EVERY PART OF THE
BODY IN TAIJI QUAN

第三节

太极运动中的呼吸配合规律及要求
THE BASIC RULES AND REQUIREMENTS OF
BREATH IN TAIJI QUAN

第一节
太极拳的由来与流派
THE ORIGINS AND SCHOOLS OF TAIJI QUAN

太极拳是武术的主要拳种。"太极"一词源出《周易·系辞》，"易有太极，是生两仪"，含有至高、至极、无穷大之意。太极拳这个名称的取义是因为太极拳拳法变幻无穷、含义丰富，而用中国古代的"太极"、"阴阳"这一哲学理论来解释和说明。

关于太极拳的起源及其创始人，民间有几种不同的说法。根据有说服力的考证，太极拳源于明末清初。据《温县志》记载，明崇祯十四年（1641），陈王廷任河南温县"乡兵守备"，明亡后隐居家乡耕田习拳，如《遗词》所说："闷来时造拳，忙来时耕田，趁余闲，教下些弟子儿孙，成龙成虎任方便……"从陈王廷的《拳经总歌》中可以了解到，他所创造的太极拳受明朝将军戚继光所编著的《拳经三十二势》的影响很大。陈王廷将《拳经三十二势》中的二十九势编入了太极拳套路，如《拳经三十二势》以"懒扎衣"为起式，而太极拳各套路起式也均以该动作为起式，甚至陈王廷《拳谱》和《拳经总歌》的文辞也与《拳经三十二势》相仿。

太极拳虽受戚继光《拳经三十二势》影响，但有其独特的风格和作用。陈王廷研究了道家的《黄庭经》，将太极拳中的手法、眼法、身法、步法的协调动作与导引、吐纳有机地结合起来。在练习时，要求意识、呼吸和动作三者密切合为一体，这就使太极拳成为内外统一的拳术运动，太极拳运用传统中医经络学说，拳势动作采用螺旋缠绕式的伸缩旋转方法，要求以腰为轴，内气发源于丹田，通过意念引导，到达任督两脉和周身，从而达到"以意用气，以气运身"的境界。

陈王廷创造的太极拳推手方法具有很强的技击性，对发展耐力、速度和灵敏度等素质都具有很大的作用。

太极拳在其长期演变过程中形成了许多不同风格和特点的传统流派，其中流传较广和具有代表性的有五式，即：陈式、杨式、吴式、武式、孙式。

从20世纪50年代开始，太极拳得到蓬勃发展。先后有二十四式、四十八式、三十二式拳剑等太极拳套路问世。90年代，又有四十二式太极拳和各式流派的太极拳竞赛套路出现。为满足全民健身需求，八式和十六式的简化型太极拳得到了推广。同时，中国传统的太极拳运动在世界各地也得到了广泛的传播。

Taiji Quan is one of the most famous Chinese traditional martial arts. The word "Taiji" comes from *Zhouyi·Xici* with the meaning of the highest, the farthest and infinite. Its theory is based on traditional Chinese philosophy.

There are different versions of its beginning and its initiator. Now people generally believe that Taiji Quan made its debut by Chen Wangting, a garrison commander in Wenxian county, Henan province in late Ming and early Qing dynasty.

Applying the theory in Jingluo in traditional Chinese medicine, all the movements take such shapes as an arc or a spiral. Every movement of the limbs calls for close co-ordination with the waist. Qi arises from Dantian, reaches the pulses of Ren and Du, and spreads to the whole body.

The form of pushing hands created by Chen Wangting emphasizes attack and defense. By practising pushing hands, one can greatly improve his or her stamina, rapidity and agility.

During the long time of development, Taiji Quan came to be associated with different families in China. These family names came to designate the different schools of Taiji Quan. There are five major schools in Taiji Quan: Chen-style, Yang-style, Wu-style, Wu-style, Sun-style.

Taiji Quan has been developing greatly. Since 1950s, a number of different sets have been established, including 24-form, 48-form, 32-form Taiji Quan, 42-form Taiji Quan as well as the simplified 8-form and 16-form Taiji Quan. Now Taiji Quan is spreading world widely, and there is a large population practising Taiji Quan all over the world.

第二节
练习太极拳对身体各部位的要求
THE REQUIREMENTS OF BODY POSTURES IN TAIJI QUAN

一、虚灵顶颈竖项
Head Erect and Neck Vertical

　　练习太极拳时要求头顶部百会穴轻轻上提，好似头顶上有绳索悬着，从而感觉有"虚灵顶颈"之意，也称"顶头悬"。虚灵顶颈可使头部自然垂直，有利于练拳时控制平衡和中枢神经对器官机能的调节等。

　　要保持虚灵顶颈姿势不松塌和不强硬，颈项要端正竖起，颈项的自然放松竖起能使头部左右转动时自然灵活，达到头正、顶平。做到虚灵顶颈，才能精神饱满、意气贯注，保持练习时动作的沉稳和扎实。

In order to keep balance, head movements in Taiji Quan must be head erect and neck vertical, as if head were hung by a thread with neck relaxed.

二、沉肩坠肘坐腕
Lowering Shoulders and Elbows Relaxing Wrist

　　练太极拳时在松肩的前提下要求沉肩和坠肘，沉肩坠肘有利于躯干的含胸拔背，同时会使人有身体重心下沉的内劲感觉。沉肩坠肘动作要保持腋下的回旋余地，不要把臂紧贴胸部或体侧，还要有微向前合抱的感觉。

坐腕的腕关节向手背一侧自然屈起，在定势动作和运转动作中都须注意坐腕要求。坐腕对各类手法的劲力都有积极作用，如腕部松懈则前臂无力。掌握自然伸展的舒指与坐腕相配合，既有动作形象美感，又有臂部的劲力体现。

When practising Taiji Quan, one should relax shoulders naturally. Don't shrug and raise elbows or closely attach elbows to ribs. The movements of wrists should be soft and steadily with power in palms.

三、含胸拔背实腹
Back and Chest Naturally Erect, Abdomen Breathing

太极拳的"含胸拔背"是一种身体基本姿势要求，不是随动作变化而变动的。它既能使胸腔上下径拉长，横膈肌有更大向下舒展余地，有利于腹式呼吸的深长，又有助于身体重心的下沉。拔背是当胸向内微含时，背部肌肉往下松沉，脊背鼓起上提，使背部肌肉产生一定张力和弹性。

横膈肌运动所产生的腹式呼吸，使腹部肌肉逐步得到锻炼，腹部渐渐充实圆满，尤其是下腹部的充实，更有益于气沉丹田的要求。腹部随练习会时松时紧，但应始终保持松静的状态和感觉。含胸拔背实腹相互作用，要求练拳时保持躯干中正姿势。

Within the whole practise, keep back and chest relaxed. Don't protrude chest or draw abdomen in. Use abdomen breathing to make Qi (air) sink into Dantian.

四、松腰敛臀圆裆
Waist Relaxing and Buttocks in Slightly

腰是身体转动的关键部位，对动作变化、重心稳定等都起主要作用。练习时，对腰部的要求是松而沉。腰部松沉时要注意使腰部直竖，以有利于尾闾中正的要求。虽然太极拳流派风格不一，如吴式太极拳的野马分鬃动作，身体姿势倾斜，但仍保持腰部脊柱直竖，也称做斜中寓直。

敛臀是在松腰的基础上使臀部稍做内收，同时和含胸拔背互相作用。敛臀时，放松臀部和腰部肌肉，使臀部肌肉向外下方舒展，然后向前、向内收敛，好似臀部把小腹托起。此举有利于气沉丹田的要求。

当两胯撑开，两膝有微向里扣的感觉时，就能起到圆裆的作用。髋关节是协调腰腿动作的主要关节，如果髋关节紧张，腰腿就很难相顺相随。圆裆和松胯的互相配合能使腰部灵活，起到臀部内敛的作用。

Waist is the axis of upper body for turning or twisting, and it can help practicers keep body balance and make movements harmonious. Waist should be relaxed with buttocks slightly in so that Qi can sink into Dantian.

五、心静体松意专
Calmness, Relaxation and Concentration

太极拳练习的重要原则是心静体松意专。也就是说，练拳时思想集中，肢体放松，以意念引导动作的变化和运行。心静体松意专要求在未练拳之前即肢体放松，端正姿势，思想上摒除其他杂念干扰，处于无思无意状态。动作开始后，更应精神集中，用意念来引导动作，做到以意导体，意动形随。需要强调的是，体松并非肢体绵软无力。所谓体松，就是要避免拙力和肢体僵硬，按照动作的虚实变化，做到全身不该用力之处不用力，逐步达到以松入柔，积柔成刚，刚柔相济。体松是一种练习太极拳时达到刚柔相济的手段和方法。

Calmness and relaxation are basic requirements for practising Taiji Quan. One should be calm and pay more attention to the movements, with the whole body relaxed. The point is relaxed but not slack, with consciousness rather than force commanding the body.

六、呼吸深长自然
Natural, Long and Deep Breath

　　练习太极拳时的呼吸，采用腹式呼吸来加深呼与吸的深长。腹式呼吸应配以意识引导动作，自然和均匀地、有意识地将气送至小腹部，也就是常说的"气沉丹田"。

　　太极拳练习的身体基本姿势都促使腹式呼吸达到深长的要求。"拳式呼吸"一般是指练习时动作的开合屈伸、起落进退、虚实变化等结合一呼一吸。掌握正确动作自然相配合的腹式呼吸方法，可使练习时肢体更放松，注意力更集中，动作更圆活和沉稳。

　　Natural breathing means a natural, long, equable and deep breath according to the certain movement. It can only be reached in terms of basic body posture of Taiji Quan.

七、势势意连形随
The Combination of Conciousness and Movements

　　太极拳讲究"一动无不有动"，而且始终以意念引导动作。每当一个动作完成时，意念中就有下一个动作出现，要有意连形随的感觉。例如两手向前按时，先要有向前按的意向，然后动作随即跟着前去。意念不中断，上一个动作和下一个动作之间不产生停顿，保持着势势相连，绵绵不断。整个套路练习从头到尾给人一种连贯圆活的感觉，又好似有行云流水的舒畅感。太极拳练习基本上是缓慢的匀速运动，在意念领先的前提下，通过不断练习，能够达到势势意连形随的境地。

　　Taiji Quan requires wholeness in actions and also requires using consciousness to control body. Its movements should be made continuous, smooth, harmonious and co-ordinated.

太极拳是一种轻灵、缓慢、沉稳的拳术。动作如抽丝般徐缓不躁，又稳又静；迈步如猫行般轻起轻落，起步和落步都要有轻灵的感觉，即所谓一举一动，周身都要轻灵，故有"运劲如抽丝、迈步如猫行"之说。轻灵和沉稳是相对独立而又统一的。太极拳的基本身体姿势和具有气沉丹田要求的腹式呼吸使身体重心下沉，无论是行步还是定势，步型、步法都要求既轻灵又沉稳。

太极拳以阴阳转换理论作指导，在每一势和每一动中，始终有着阴阳转换，即虚与实的转换。例如云手，左脚虚右脚实时，左脚向侧跨步；左脚实右脚虚时，右脚向左脚并步。身体重心也随着步型、步法的虚实变化而不断转换位置，不会有滞迟沉重的感觉。同时虚实的变化应贯穿于整个套路之中。

阴阳本身就是一对矛盾，而不断地转换就形成了不停顿的运动。太极拳的轻灵、沉稳、虚涵、扎实也在不断的练习过程中转换和变化，逐步达到统一和谐的境地。

Lightness means when practising Taiji Quan, your steps should be as light as a cat's walking. Heaviness means the basic posture of Taiji Quan requires the sinking of body weight as well as Qi sinking into Dantian.

Taiji Quan is based on the theory of Yi Yang. Yin means emptiness; Yang means solidness. When your left foot is empty, the right one must be solid. Within the whole practising, emptiness and solidness change into each other without stopping.

第三节
太极运动中的呼吸配合规律及要求
THE BASIC RULES AND REQUIREMENTS OF
BREATH IN TAIJI QUAN

　　练习太极拳可以分为三个阶段。第一阶段，主要是把握姿势，学会动作，把套路中的步型、步法、腿法、身型、手型、手法、眼神等基本要求弄清楚，做到姿势正确、步伐稳定、动作舒展、招式连贯。简单地说就是"记忆阶段"。第二个阶段，应是掌握动作的变化规律及其特点，提高上下肢的配合、眼与手的配合、左与右的配合等外部形体的协调配合能力及其技巧。第三个阶段，主要练习重点则是提高呼吸与动作的配合能力。学会呼吸与动作的配合技巧，才能真正体验到太极拳运动的健身价值。

When learning Taiji Quan, we should practise it step by step. Generally speaking, there are three steps in learning Taiji Quan. Step one, form correct body postures and the postures of upper limbs and lower limbs. In this step, pay more attention to body postures and the basic movements of arms and hands, legs and feet as well as eyes so as to make your body postures correct and movements smooth and steadily. Step two, improve the harmony of movements between upper limbs and lower limbs, eyes and hands, left and right, understand the basic rules and the characteristics of the techniques in Taiji Quan. Step three, emphasize the co-operation of breath and movements. Learn how to breathe when practising Taiji Quan. Breathing properly can greatly increase the effects on keeping fit and curing diseases.

　　呼吸配合动作是太极拳运动的真正意义所在。练习太极拳如果不懂得呼吸配合，只是一种动作缓慢的广播操，其锻炼价值和健身效果并不明显。太极拳的运动速度与练习者的呼吸频率紧密相连，呼吸频率快，则运动速度就快；呼吸频率慢，运动速度就缓慢。也就是说，每个人的呼吸频率不同，练拳的速度就不该相同，所以，按照音乐口令练习太极拳或比赛，其实是对太极拳练习的误导。

Different from some other setting-up exercises, Taiji Quan emphasizes the harmonization of breath and movements. It is essential for Taiji Quan lovers to understand this. The functions of Taiji Quan practising arise from it. Different people have different breathing frequency. The pace of movements lies on the pace of breath, thus different people should have different pace of movements. It is a kind of misunderstanding that we should practise Taiji Quan at a fixed pace.

太极拳中的呼吸是根据动作的开合伸展、起落进退、虚实变化等结合一呼和一吸，例如，两臂慢慢向前平举时要吸气，而身体下蹲、两臂下落时则要呼气。这种呼吸方式是根据胸廓张缩和膈肌活动的变化、在符合动作要求与生理需要的基础上进行的。我们称之为"拳式呼吸"。

The breath in Taiji Quan should be co-operated with the movements closely. For example, inhale when raising arms upward; exhale when lowering body weight or arms. We call this way of breathing "Quan-style breathing".

太极拳是一种"运动着的气功"，吸呼配合是太极拳练习的基本要求，而注重呼吸的目的在于意念集中，集中意念的目的在于入静，只有入静之后练太极，才能达到太极的至高境界，收到神奇的健身效果。所以学会呼吸配合技巧是进入太极至高境界的入门介质。

下面我们介绍呼吸与动作配合的几种规律：

Taiji Quan is a kind of "motional Chikung". The co-operation of breathing and movements is a basic requirement of Taiji Quan. Proper breath leads to concentration, concentration results in mental calmness. It is the highest level of Taiji Quan to practise it with inner calmness.

The following is some basic rules of breathing in Taiji Quan.

一、起吸落呼
Inhale when Rising, Exhale when Decending

序图1

序图2

根据动作的起伏、升降进行呼吸配合。一般情况下，身体重心或局部肢体向上起升时吸气，向下降落时呼气。比如："起式"，两臂向前上举起时吸气，两手向下落、重心下沉时呼气。（序图1、序图2）再比如："上步"，提脚迈步时吸气，脚跟落地时呼气。（序图3、序图4）

Generally speaking, inhale when body weight or a part of body rising; exhale when they lowering. For example, "starting posture", inhale when raising arms upward; exhale when lowering body weight and pressing hands downward. (Picture 1, Picture 2) "step forward", inhale when lifting a foot and stepping forward; exhale when landing the foot. (Picture 3, Picture 4)

序图3

序图4

二、开吸合呼
Inhale when Opening, Exhale when Closing

根据动作的伸缩、收放进行呼吸配合。一般情况下两臂向外张开的动作要吸气，两臂向内合抱的动作要呼气。比如："开合手"，两手向外张开时吸气，两手向内合挤时呼气。（序图5～序图7）再比如："抱球"，两手上下划弧时吸气，两手向内合抱时呼气。（序图8～序图10）

Commonly, inhale when arms extending; exhale when drawing hands back, such as "opening and closing hands". (Picture 5 - Picture 7) For example, "holding a ball", inhale when arms moving upward or downward in an arc; exhale when arms "holding a ball". (Picture 8 - Picture 10)

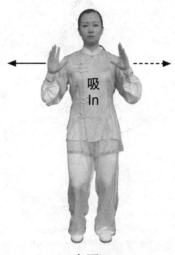

序图5

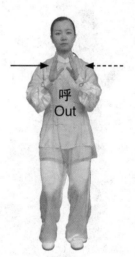

序图6

序图7

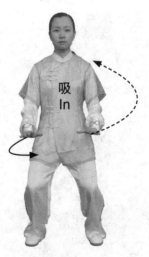

序图8

序图9

序图10

序图11

序图12

序图13

三、进吸退呼
Inhale when Stepping Forward, Exhale when Stepping Backward

　　根据动作的前进、后退进行呼吸配合。一般情况下，身体重心向前移动时吸气，重心后坐时呼气。比如："野马分鬃"，重心前移弓步时吸气，重心向后坐时呼气。（序图11～序图13）

Commonly, inhale when body weight moving forward; exhale when it sitting back. For example, "Parting the Wild Horse's Mane", inhale when moving body weight forward to form bow step, exhale when sitting back. (Picture 11 - Picture 13)

四、发力动作的呼吸规律
Rules of Breathing when Using Explosive Strength

在太极运动中有许多爆发用力和突然制动的动作，这类动作的呼吸配合要求以短促呼气或"屏气"来配合。比如："掩手肱捶"，在冲拳的一刹那配合短促的呼气，以气助力。（序图14、序图15）

呼＋屏气
Out and Hold

序图14

The movements in Taiji Quan are usually slow and continuous, but there are some movements with the features of explosive strength and sudden stopping. When practising the movements, we should use short exhaling, or "holding breath". For example, "Cover Hands and Strike with Fist", punching with a short exhaling, which makes the punching more powerful. (Picture 14, Picture 15)

序图15

序图16

五、技击方法的呼吸规律
The Rules of Breathing in the Fighting Skills of Taiji Quan and Taiji Sword

1. "掤"（pēng）
Pushing

前臂由下向前、向上掤出时要配合呼气。（序图16）

Exhale when the arm in front pushes forward. (Picture 16)

2. "捋"
Stroke

捋的动作开始前先要吸气，当双手向下、向后捋时要配合呼气。（序图17～序图19）

Inhale before starting the movement; exhale when pulling both hands down and back. (Picture 17 - Picture 19)

序图17

序图18

序图19

3. "挤"
Squeezing

挤的动作开始前，两手先要上提，此时吸气；当双手向前挤出时要配合呼气。（序图20~序图22）

Before starting the movement, inhale when lifting hands; exhale when pressing hands forward. (Picture 20 - Picture 22)

序图20

序图21

序图22

4. "按"
Pressing

双手由前向后回抽时吸气，当双手向下、向前按推时要配合呼气。（序图23~序图25）

Inhale when drawing hands back; exhale when pushing hands down and forward. (Picture 23 - Picture 25)

序图23

序图24

序图25

呼
Out

序图26

吸
In

序图27

5. "刺剑"
Thrusting Sword

在太极剑法中，刺剑时要配合呼气。（序图26）

Exhale when thrusting sword. (Picture 26)

6. "抽剑"
Drawing Sword Back

当剑由远端向近端、由前向后回抽时，要配合吸气。（序图27、序图28）

Inhale when drawing sword back. (Picture 27, Picture 28)

7. "架剑"
Blocking Sword

当剑由下向上、由低向高架起时，要配合吸气。（序图29、序图30）

Inhale when moving the sword upward. (Picture 29, Picture 30)

8. "劈剑"
Chopping Sword

当剑由上向下劈砍时，要配合呼气。（序图31、序图32）

Exhale when chopping sword downward. (Picture 31, Picture 32)

序图28

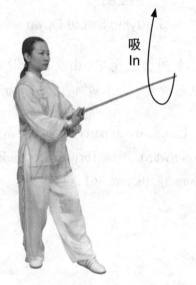

序图29

序图30

序图31

序图32

吸
In

序图33

9. "上撩剑"
Cutting Sword Up

当剑由下向上、由后下向前上撩起时，要配合吸气。
（序图33、序图34）

Inhale when cutting sword from lower back to upper front.(Picture 33, Picture 34)

10. "下挂剑"
Parrying Sword Down

当剑由上向下、由前向后挂拨时，要配合呼气。（序图35、序图36）

Exhale when parrying sword from top to downward, from forward to backward. (Picture 35, Picture 36)

序图34

呼
Out

序图35

序图36

11. "崩剑" 和 "抖剑"
Tilting Sword

在陈式太极剑法中有许多需要发力抖劲的剑法。如"平崩剑"和"马步推剑"等，这类剑法的呼吸要求配合短促的呼气，以气助力。（序图37～序图40）

There are a lot of movements with explosive strength in Chen-style Taiji Sword, such as "tilt sword" and "push sword in horse-riding step". Exhale when doing these movements. (Picture 37 - Picture 40)

呼＋屏气
Out and Hold

序图37

序图38

呼＋屏气
Out and Hold

序图39

序图40

以上所述，是太极运动中呼吸与动作配合的一般规律，在练习中准确地呼吸配合，能使练习者收到事半功倍的锻炼效果。需要指出的是，不是每次练习都能准确无误地按照规律正确地配合呼与吸，呼吸配合的准确率会随着太极练习素养的不断提升而逐步提高。在掌握呼吸配合的一般规律之后，还要在特定动作组合中灵活运用，切不可死搬教条，生搬硬套，以免对身体造成伤害。练习者应在长期的练拳实践中用心体会，不断提高。

The above are just general rules of breathing in Taiji Quan. It is impossible for a learner to learn it well without mistakes at the beginning. Your breathing skill will be improved step by step through hard work and with continuous practise. On the other hand, the above rules should be used flexibly according to a certain movement, instead of being used dogmatically.

ILLUSTRATIONS AND BREATHING TECHNIQUES

第一节

24式太极拳呼吸配合法简介

BRIEF INTRODUCTION OF BREATHING METHOD OF 24 FORM TAIJI QUAN

第二节

24式太极拳呼吸配合法动作名称

MOVEMENT NAMES OF BREATHING METHOD OF 24 FORM TAIJI QUAN

第三节

24式太极拳呼吸配合方法说明

EXPLANATIONS OF BREATHING METHOD OF 24 FORM TAIJI QUAN

第二章 动作分解与呼吸配合法

第一节
24式太极拳呼吸配合法简介
BRIEF INTRODUCTION OF BREATHING
METHOD OF 24 FORM TAIJI QUAN

　　24式太极拳呼吸配合法是一种与众不同的太极拳术，它主要讲解动作如何配合呼吸的练习方法，以及太极拳练习中的意念导引方法，是太极运动中高级训练教程。

　　呼吸配合和意念导引是太极拳具有神奇健身功效的关键所在，本书详细介绍每一个动作的呼吸方法、呼吸要领和呼吸规律，它将带领您进入真正的太极练习境界，并会收到意想不到的健身效果。这套拳法具有中正自然、舒展大方、均匀连贯的特点，同时也规范了一些不同练法，此拳术是经过国家武术权威机构审定的普及推广套路。

　　本书采用图文教材与影视教材相结合的立体教学手段，并邀请此拳法权威人士进行技术表演和教学示范，保证学习者获取原汁原味的技法传承。

The Breathing Method of 24 Form Taiji Quan is one of the spectacular Taiji boxing styles. It mainly explains the exercise method on how movement matches up with breathing, and the method of consciousness guidance in Taiji Quan exercise. It is the advanced training course in "Taiji" sport.

Respiratory tie and consciousness guidance is the key reason why Taiji Quan has magical health-building function. The book introduces in details breathing method, essentials and regular pattern of each movement. It will bring you to a genuine "Taiji" exercise realm, and produce unexpected effect of fitness. The fist position has the features of generous stretch and uniform continuity, and standardizes different exercise methods. Th Chinese shadow boxing is the universal, popularized set pattern after the validation of national wushu authority.

 This book adopts the three-dimensional teaching method of the combination of diagram, words and video. The authoritative are invited for technical performance and teaching demonstrations, guaranteeing the learners to gain the real technical method transmission.

第二节
24式太极拳呼吸配合法动作名称
MOVEMENT NAMES OF BREATHING
METHOD OF 24 FORM TAIJI QUAN

一、起式 　　　　　　The Starting Form

二、左右野马分鬃 　　Parting the Wild Horse's Mane R and L

三、白鹤亮翅 　　　　White Crane Spreads Its Wings

四、左右搂膝拗步 　　Brush Knee and Twist Step R and L

五、手挥琵琶 　　　　Hand Strums the Lute

六、倒卷肱 　　　　　Step Back and Whirl Arm on Both Sides

七、左揽雀尾 　　　　Grasp the Peacock's Tail Left

八、右揽雀尾 　　　　Grasp the Peacock's Tail Right

九、单鞭 　　　　　　Dan Bian

十、云手 　　　　　　Wave Hands

十一、单鞭 　　　　　Dan Bian

十二、高探马 　　　　Pat High on the Horse

十三、右蹬脚 　　　　Kick with Right Leg

十四、双峰贯耳 　　　Strike Opponent's Ears with Both Fists

十五、转身左蹬脚 　　Kick with Left Leg

十六、左下势独立 　　Push Down and Stand on Left Leg

十七、右下势独立 　　Push Down and Stand on Right Leg

第三节
24式太极拳呼吸配合方法说明
EXPLANATIONS OF BREATHING
METHOD OF 24 FORM TAIJI QUAN

图1

图2

一、起式
The Starting Form

1. 身体直立，两脚开立，
   与肩同宽，脚尖向前，
   两臂下垂，目视前方。
   （图1）

Stand upright with feet apart as wide
as shoulder, toes pointing forward, arms
hanging naturally at sides. Look at forward.
(Fig 1)

2. 两臂上抬，成前平举，
   手与肩平，手心向下。
   （图2、图3）

Raise arms slowly forward to shoulders
level with palms down and arms naturally
straight. (Fig 2, Fig 3)

3. 上体正直，屈膝下蹲，
   两掌下按，目视前方。
   （图4）

Keep torso erect, bend knees while pressing palms down gently with elbows low and shoulders relaxed. Look at forward. (Fig 4)

〖呼吸配合〗
[Breathing Method]

两脚开立之后，先做深呼吸一次。然后两手上提时吸气，两手下按时呼气，并配合两腿缓慢下蹲。（图1～图4）

Take a deep breath when standing with feet together. Then inhale when raising arms upward, and exhale when pressing hands down with both knees bending. (Fig 1 - Fig 4)

图3

图4

二、左右野马分鬃
Parting the Wild Horse' Mane R and L

1. 上体右转，重心右移，
   右手平屈，手心向下，
   左手划弧，手心向上，
   两手相对，成抱球状，
   左脚内收，至右脚侧，
   脚尖点地，眼看右手。
   （图5）

图5

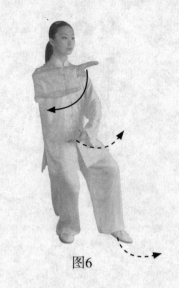

图6

Turn torso slightly to right with body weight shifting onto right leg. Bend right arm horizontally to the front of right chest with palm facing down, at the same time, left hand moves at the right and bottom in an arc till it comes under right hand, with palm facing up. Both palms face each other as if hold a ball. Left foot moves to right foot with toe touching ground slightly beside right instep. Look at right hand. (Fig 5)

2. 上体左转，左脚迈出，
   成左弓步，上体左转，
   左手左上，与眼平齐，
   右手右下，手心向下，
   眼看左手。（图6～图8）

图7

Torso turns slightly to left. Left foot takes a step forward to left with heel touching ground. Shift weight onto left leg with left knee bending and right leg straight, making a left bow stance. Keep turning torso while raising left hand to eyes level with palm facing up and elbow slightly bending, and lowering right hand to the side of right hip with palm facing down and fingers pointing forward. Look at left hand. (Fig 6 - Fig 8)

图8

3. 身体后坐，重心右移，
   左脚翘起，微向外撇，
   逐渐踏实，成左弓步，
   身体左转，重心左移，
   左手向下，胸前平屈，
   右手划弧，至左手下，
   两手相对，成抱球状，
   右脚内收，至左脚侧，
   脚尖点地，眼看左手。
   （图9～图11）

图9

Torso moves backward slowly, body weight shifts onto right leg with right knee bending and left toe lifting. Then left toe turns outward before placing left sole firmly on ground. Turn torso to left, bend left knee with body weight shifting onto left leg, bend left arm horizontally to the front of left chest with palm facing down, move right hand to left at waist level, with palm facing up and left palm on top as if hold a ball, at the same time, take right foot to inner side of left instep, toe touching ground slightly. Look at left hand. (Fig 9 - Fig 11)

图10

图11

图12

图13

图14

4. 右腿迈出，成右弓步，
   上体右转，双肘微屈，
   向前挤出，眼看右手。
   （图12、图13）

Take a step towards right with right foot, right heel touching ground first before placing right sole firmly on ground. Turn torso to right with body weight shifting onto right leg, right knee bends and left leg straight, making a right bow stance. At the same time, right hand moves forward and up to eyes level with palm facing up, left hand moves downward to the side of left hip with palms facing down and fingers pointing forward. Look at right hand. (Fig 12, Fig 13)

5. 身体后坐，重心左移，
   右脚翘起，微向外撇，
   逐渐踏实，成右弓步，
   身体右转，重心右移，
   右手向下，胸前平屈，
   左手划弧，至右手下，
   手心相对，成抱球状，
   左脚内收，至右脚侧，
   脚尖点地，眼看右手。
   （图14～图16）

Take a step towards left with left foot, left heel touching ground first before placing left sole firmly on ground.

Turn torso to left with body weight shifting onto left leg, left knee bends and right leg straight, making a left bow stance. At the same time, left hand moves forward and up to eyes level with palm facing up, right hand moves downward to the side of right hip with palms facing down and fingers pointing forward. Look at left hand. (Fig 14 - Fig 16)

图15

6. 左腿迈出，成左弓步，
   上体左转，右手左下，
   左手右上，双肘微屈，
   右手下落，至右胯旁，
   手心向下，指尖向前，
   眼看左手。（图17、图18）

图16

Take a step towards left with right foot, left heel touching ground first before placing left sole firmly on ground. Turn torso to left with body weight shifting onto left leg, left knee bends and right leg straight, making a left bow stance. At the same time, left hand moves forward and up to eyes level with palm facing up, right hand moves downward to the side of right hip with palms facing down and fingers pointing forward. Look at left hand. (Fig 17, Fig 18)

图17

【呼吸配合】
[Breathing Method]

在这个动作过程中共有3次"抱球"和3次"分鬃"。从"抱球"动作开始，右手上提时吸气，两手合抱时呼气。向前弓步时（分鬃）吸气，向后移重心（后坐）时呼气，其中过渡动作"抱球"时，要先吸后呼。（图5～图18）

In this series, you should repeat the movements of "hold a ball" and "part the wild horse's mane on both sides" alternately three times each. Starting from "hold a ball" posture, inhale when raising right arm; exhale when "two hands like holding a ball". Inhale when making a bow stance; exhale when shifting body weight backwards. (Fig 5 - Fig 18)

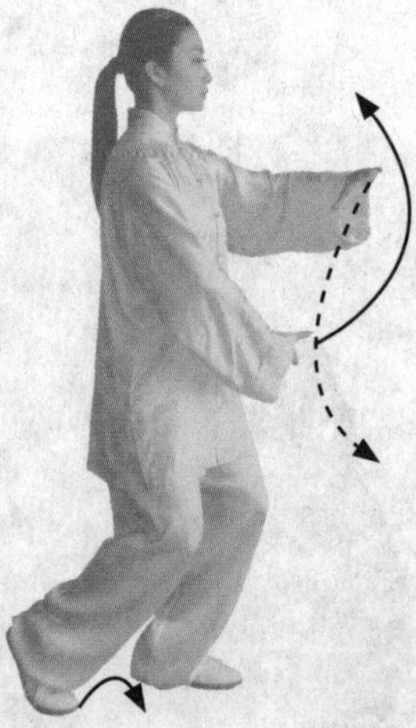

图18

三、白鹤亮翅
White Crane Spreads Its Wings

1. 上体左转，左臂平屈，置于胸前，右手划弧，成抱球状，眼看左手。
（图19）

Turn torso slightly to left. Turn both hands over with left palm above facing down and right palm under facing up as if hold a ball. Look at left hand. (Fig 19)

图19

2. 右脚跟进，上体后坐，
重心右移，左脚前移，
脚尖点地，成左虚步，
右手上提，于右额前，
左手下落，于左胯前，
双目平视。（图20、图21）

Take a half step forward with right foot to the back of left foot. Shift body weight onto right leg while torso turning slightly to right. Look at right hand. Then move left foot a bit forward with toe touching ground slightly. Both knees bend to make a left empty stance. At the same time, turn torso slightly to left, facing forward, with hands parting to upper right and lower left separately until right hand in front of right temple, palm facing to left ear, and left hand beside left hip, palm facing down, fingers pointing forward. Look at level of front. (Fig 20, Fig 21)

图20

【呼吸配合】
[Breathing Method]

接上一动作，右脚跟半步，两手腹前"抱球"时呼气，右手上提"亮翅"时吸气，左脚向前点地时呼气，并配合沉肩坠肘腹部放松气沉丹田。（图19～图21）

Exhale when moving right foot forward in a half step, and "hold a ball" in front of the abdomen. Inhale when raising right hand upward "to show the wings". Exhale when placing left foot in front of right foot with left toe touching ground. (Fig 19 - Fig 21)

图21

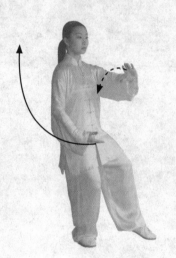

图22

图23

四、左右搂膝拗步
Brush Knee and Twist Step R and L

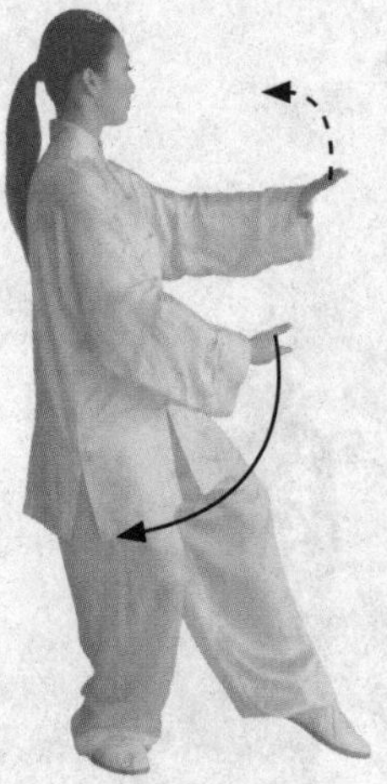

1. 右手下落，至右肩外，
   左手划弧，至右胸前，
   手心斜下，上体右转，
   左脚内收，至右脚侧，
   脚尖点地，眼看右手。
   （图22～图24）

Torn torso slightly to left, move right hand downward and left hand upward. Then turn torso to right. Following torso turning, right hand rows an arc passing abdomen and upward to ear level, with left hand moving in an upward arc, and then in a downward arc to the front of right chest, palm facing down. At the same time, left foot moving back to the inner side of right instep with toe touching ground. Look at right hand. (Fig 22 - Fig 24)

图24

2. 上体左转，左脚前迈，
  成左弓步，右手屈肘，
  经由耳侧，向前推出，
  高与鼻平，左手向下，
  搂过左膝，落左膝旁，
  指尖向前，眼看右手。
  （图25、图26）

Turn torso to left, left foot takes a step
in that direction for a left bow stance. At
the same time, right hand draws leftward
passing right ear, and following body
turning, pushes forward at nose level with
palm facing forward. While left hand rows
an arc around left knee to lie beside left
hip, palm downward. Look at right hand.
(Fig 25, Fig 26)

图25

3. 右腿屈膝，上体后坐，
  重心右移，左脚翘起，
  微向外撇，逐渐踏实，
  左腿前弓，身体左转，
  重心左移，右脚内收，
  至左脚侧，脚尖点地，
  左手外翻，经由左后，
  向上划弧，至左肩外，
  右手划弧，置左胸前，
  手心斜下，眼看左手。
  （图27～图29）

Sit back slowly with right knee bending.
Shift weight onto right leg. Raise toe of
left foot and turn it a bit outward before
placing whole foot on ground. Then bend
left leg and turn torso slightly to left, shift
weight onto left leg. Right foot steps

图26

图27

图28

forward to the side of left foot, toe on ground. At the same time, turn left palm up and with elbow slightly bending, move left hand sideways and up to shoulder level while right hand follows body turning, moves upward, leftward, downward curve to the front of the left part of chest, with palm facing obliquely downward. Look at left hand. (Fig 27 - Fig 29)

4. 上体右转，右脚前迈，
　　成右弓步，左手屈肘，
　　经由耳侧，向前推出，
　　高与鼻平，右手向下，
　　搂过右膝，落右膝旁，
　　指尖向前，眼看左手。
　　（图30、图31）

图29

Turn torso to right, right foot takes a step in that direction for a right bow stance. At the same time, left hand draws rightward passing left ear, and following body turning, pushes forward at nose level with palm facing forward; while right hand rows an arc around right knee to lie beside right hip, palm downward. Look at left hand. (Fig 30, Fig 31)

5. 左腿屈膝，上体后坐，
　　重心左移，右脚翘起，
　　微向外撇，逐渐踏实，
　　右腿前弓，身体右转，
　　重心右移，左脚内收，
　　至右脚侧，脚尖点地，
　　右手外翻，经由右后，
　　向上划弧，至右肩外，

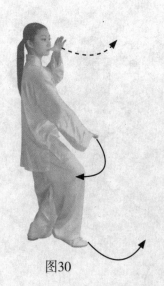

图30

左手划弧，置右胸前，
手心斜下，眼看右手。
（图32～图34）

Sit back slowly with left knee bending.
Shift weight onto left leg. Raise toe of
right foot and turn it a bit outward before
placing whole foot on ground. Then bend
right leg and turn torso slightly to right,
shift weight onto right leg. Left foot steps
forward to the side of right foot toe on
ground. At the same time, turn right palm
up with elbow slightly bending, move
right hand sideways and up to shoulder
level while left hand follows body turning,
moves upward, rightward, downward
curve to the front of the right part of chest,
with palm facing obliquely downward.
Look at right hand. (Fig 32 - Fig 34)

图31

图32

图33

图34

6. 上体左转，左脚前迈，
成左弓步，右手屈肘，
经由耳侧，向前推出，
高与鼻平，左手向下，
搂过左膝，落左膝旁，
指尖向前，眼看右手。
（图35、图36）

Turn torso to left, left foot takes a step in that direction for a left bow stance. At the same time, right hand draws leftward passing right ear, and following body turning, pushes forward at nose level with palm facing forward; while left hand circles around left knee to lie beside left hip, palm downward. Look at right hand. (Fig 35, Fig 36)

图35

【呼吸配合】
[Breathing Method]

转身划弧时吸气，向前弓步搂手推掌时呼气。（图22～图36）

Inhale when turning body rows an arc and brushing knee; exhale when step forward to form a bow step with pushing hand forward. (Fig 22 - Fig 36)

图36

五、手挥琵琶
Hand Strums the Lute

右脚向前，跟进半步，
上体后坐，重心右移，

左脚提起，稍向前移，
成左虚步，脚跟着地，
脚尖翘起，左手挑举，
高与鼻平，掌心向右，
左臂微屈，右手收回，
置左肘侧，掌心向左，
眼看左手。（图37～图39）

Right foot takes half a step towards left heel. Sit back and turn torso slightly to right, shift weight onto right leg. Lift left foot and move it forward, with heel touching ground and knee bends a little for a left empty stance. At the same time, raise left hand in an arc to nose level, with palm facing rightward and elbow slightly bends, right hand moves to the inside of left elbow, with palm facing leftward. Look at left hand. (Fig 37 - Fig 39)

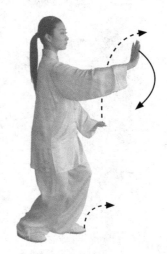

图37

【 呼吸配合 】
[Breathing Method]

接上一动作，右脚跟半步吸气；左脚前伸，脚跟落地时呼气。同时配合两手上提时吸气，屈臂下落时呼气。（图37～图39）

图38

Inhale when bring right foot forward in half step and raising both arms upward; exhale when extending left leg forward with left heel touching ground and dropping arms down with elbows bending. (Fig 37 - Fig 39)

图39

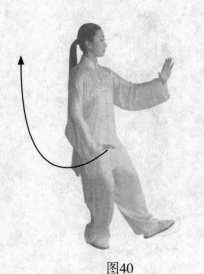

图40

六、倒卷肱
Step Back and Whirl Arm on Both Sides

1. 上体右转，右手翻掌，
   手心向上，经由腹前，
   划弧平举，双臂微屈，
   左手翻掌，手心向上，
   眼随手动，平视左手。
   （图40、图41）

Torso turns slightly to right, move right hand down in an arc passing abdomen and then upward to the level of shoulder, palm up and arm slightly bends. Turn left palm up and place left toe on ground. Eyes follow left hand and then Look at left hand. (Fig 40, Fig 41)

图41

2. 右臂屈肘，经由耳侧，
   右手前推，左臂屈肘，
   同时后撤，手心向上，
   至左肋外，左腿轻提，
   后退一步，成右虚步，
   跟随转体，眼看右手。
   （图42、图43）

Bend right arm and draw hand passing the right ear before pushing it out with the palm facing forward, left hand moves to the side of waist, palm up. At the same time, lift left foot slightly and take a curved step backward, toe touching ground first and then placing whole foot

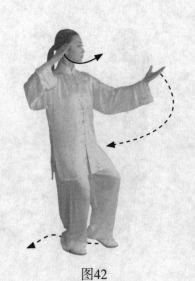

图42

on ground, body turns slightly to left and shift weight onto left leg for a right empty stance. Look at right hand. (Fig 42, Fig 43)

图43

3. 上体左转，左手划弧，
   随即平举，手心向上，
   右手翻掌，掌心向上，
   眼随体转，平视左手。
   （图44）

Turn torso slightly to left, left hand moves sideways up to shoulder level, palm up, while right palm turns up. Eyes follow left hand and then Look at left hand. (Fig 44)

图44

4. 左臂屈肘，经由耳侧，
   左手前推，右臂屈肘，
   同时后撤，手心向上，
   至右肋外，右腿轻提，
   后退一步，成左虚步，
   跟随转体，眼看左手。
   （图45、图46）

Bend left arm and draw hand passing the left ear before pushing it out with the palm facing forward, right hand moves to the side of waist, palm up. At the same time, lift right foot slightly and take a curved step backward, toe touching ground first and then placing whole foot on ground, body turns slightly to right and shift weight onto right leg for a left empty

图45

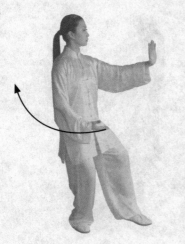

图46

stance. Look at left hand. (Fig 45, Fig 46)

5. 上体右转，右手划弧，
   随即平举，手心向上，
   左手翻掌，掌心向上，
   眼随体转，平视右手。
   （图47）

Turn torso slightly to right, right hand moves sideways up to shoulder level, palm up, while left palm turns up. Eyes follow right hand and then Look at right hand. (Fig 47)

图47

6. 右臂屈肘，经由耳侧，
   右手前推，左臂屈肘，
   同时后撤，手心向上，
   至左肋外，左腿轻提，
   后退一步，成右虚步，
   跟随体转，眼看右手。
   （图48、图49）

Bend right arm and draw hand passing the right ear before pushing it out with the palm facing forward, left hand moves to the side of waist, palm up. At the same time, lift left foot slightly and take a curved step backward, toe touching ground first and then placing whole foot on ground, body turns slightly to left and shift weight onto left leg for a right empty stance. Look at right hand. (Fig 48, Fig 49)

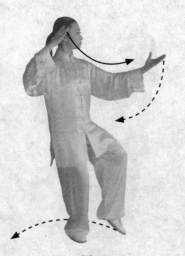

图48

7. 上体左转，左手划弧，
   随即平举，手心向上，
   右手翻掌，掌心向上，
   眼随体转，平视左手。
   （图50）

图49

Turn torso slightly to left, left hand moves sideways up to shoulder level, palm up, while right palm turns up. Eyes follow left hand and then look at left hand. (Fig 50)

8. 左臂屈肘，经由耳侧，
   左手前推，右臂屈肘，
   同时后撤，手心向上，
   至右肋外，右腿轻提，
   后退一步，成左虚步，
   跟随转体，眼看左手。
   （图51、图52）

图50

Bend left arm and draw hand passing the left ear before pushing it out with the palm facing forward, right hand moves to the side of waist, palm up. At the same time, lift right foot slightly and take a curved step backward, toe touching ground first and then placing whole foot on ground, body turns slightly to right and shift weight onto right leg for a left empty stance. Look at left hand. (Fig 51, Fig 52)

图51

图52

图53

【呼吸配合】

[Breathing Method]

两手展开时吸气，合手"卷肱"时呼气。同时配合向后退步：脚离地时吸气，当脚落地时呼气。（图40~图52）

Exhale when arms push out, inhale when doing "whirl arm on both side". At the same time, inhale when lifting foot that you step back, exhale when falling foot on the ground. (Fig 40 - Fig 52)

七、左揽雀尾
Grasp the Peacock's Tail Left

1. 上体右转，右手划弧，
   随即平举，手心向上，
   左手放松，手心向上，
   眼看左手。（图53）

Turn torso slightly to the right, right hand moves sideways up to shoulder level, palm up, while left palm turns downward, Look at left hand. (Fig 53)

2. 身体右转，左手下落，
   逐渐翻掌，腹前划弧，
   置右肋前，手心向上，
   右臂屈肘，手心向下，
   置右胸前，两手相对，
   成抱球状，重心右移，

图54

左脚内收，置右脚侧，
脚尖点地，眼看右手。
（图54、图55）

Turn body slightly to right and make
a hold-ball gesture in front of right chest,
right hand on top. At the same time, shift
weight onto right leg and draw left foot
to the inner side of right foot, with toe
touching ground. Look at right hand.
(Fig 54, Fig 55)

图55

3. 上体左转，左脚迈出，
　　成左弓步，左臂掤出，
　　高与肩平，手心向后，
　　右手下落，置右胯旁，
　　手心向下，指尖向前，
　　看左前臂。（图56、图57）

Turn body slightly to left, left foot
takes a step forward to left for a left bow
stance. Meanwhile, push out left forearm
and the back of hand up to shoulder level,
while right hand drops slowly to the side
of right hip, palm down. Look at left
forearm. (Fig 56, Fig 57)

图56

图57

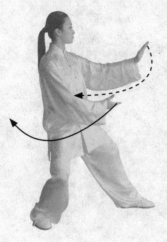

图58

4. 身体左转，左手前伸，
翻掌向下，右手翻掌，
手心向上，两手下将，
上体右转，右手划弧，
手心向上，高与肩齐，
左臂平屈，置于胸前，
重心右移，眼看右手。
（图58、图59）

Turn torso slightly to left while left
hand extends forward, palm down. Right
hand moves forward and upward until it
is below left forearm, palm up. Then turn
torso slightly to right while pulling both
hands down and back in a curve passing
abdomen until right hand extends sideways
at shoulder level, palm up, and left forearm
lies across chest, palm facing inward. At
the same time, shift weight onto right leg.
Look at right hand. (Fig 58, Fig 59)

图59

5. 上体左转，右臂屈肘，
双手相对，继续左转，
双手向前，慢慢挤出，
重心前移，成左弓步，
看左手腕。（图60、图61）

Turn torso slightly to left while
bending right arm and touching the inside
of left wrist with right palm; torso keeps
turning to right when pressing both hands
forward, palms facing each other and
continue to spin. Shift weight onto left leg

图60

for a left bow stance. Look at left wrist. (Fig 60, Fig 61)

图61

6. 两手分开，平抹下按，
   右腿屈膝，上体后坐，
   重心右移，左脚翘起，
   两手屈肘，收回腹前，
   双手手心，向前下方，
   目视前方。（图62～图64）

Turn both palms downward as right hand passes over left wrist and moves forward in a curve. Separate hands shoulder-width apart and draw them back to the front of abdomen, palms slightly downward. Then, sit back and shift weight onto right leg with knee bending, raise toe of left foot. Look forward. (Fig 62 - Fig 64)

图62

7. 上式不停，重心前移，
   两手按出，掌心向前，
   左腿弓步，目视前方。
   （图65）

Shift weight onto left leg while pushing palms upward, forward curve until hands at shoulder level. At the same time, bend left leg to make left bow stance. Look forward. (Fig 65)

图63

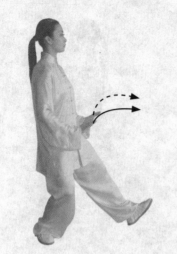

图64

图65

图66

【呼吸配合】
[Breathing Method]

从"抱球"动作开始，"抱球"时先吸后呼。然后"掤"时吸气，"捋"时呼气，"挤"前提手时吸气，向前"挤"时呼气，"按"前身体后移时吸气，两手前"按"时呼气。（图53～图65）

Starting from "hold a ball", inhale first and then exhale when doing the "hold a ball". After that, inhale when pushing left forearm forward; exhale when pulling both hands back; inhale when raising hands and exhale when pressing forward with left wrist; inhale when moving body weight backward, and exhale when pushing forward with both hands. (Fig 53 - Fig 65)

八、右揽雀尾
Grasp the Peacock's Tail Right

1. 上体后坐，身体右转，右手划弧，置于腹前，左手屈肘，置于胸前，两手相对，成抱球状，重心左移，右脚内收，至左脚侧，脚尖点地，眼看左手。（图66～图69）

图67

图68

Sit back and turn torso to right, shift weight onto right leg and turn left toe inward. Right hand moves to the right in a horizontal curve and then in a downward curve passing abdomen for a ball-holding gesture in front of left chest, with left hand above. Meanwhile, shift weight onto left leg and place right foot beside left foot, toe touching ground. Look at left hand. (Fig 66 - Fig 69)

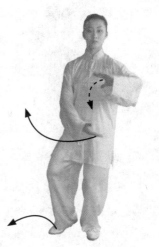

图69

2. 上体右转，右脚迈出，
   成右弓步，右臂掤出，
   高与肩平，手心向后，
   左手下落，置左胯旁，
   手心向下，指尖向前，
   看右前臂。（图70、图71）

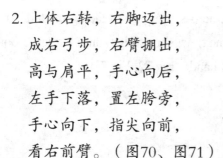

图70

图71

Turn body slightly to right, right foot takes a step forward to right for a right bow stance. Meanwhile, push out right forearm and the back of hand up to shoulder level, while left hand drops slowly to the side of left hip, palm down. Look at right forearm. (Fig 70, Fig 71)

3. 身体右转，右手下翻，
   左手翻掌，手心向上，
   两手下捋，上体左转，
   左手屈肘，高与肩齐，
   右臂平屈，置于胸前，
   重心左移，眼看左手。
   （图72、图73）

图72

Turn torso slightly to right while right hand extends forward, palm down. Left hand moves forward and upward until it is below right forearm, palm up. Then turn torso slightly to left while pulling both hands down and back in a curve past abdomen until left hand extends sideways at shoulder level, palm up, and right forearm lies across chest, palm facing inward. At the same time, shift weight onto left leg. Look at left hand. (Fig 72, Fig 73)

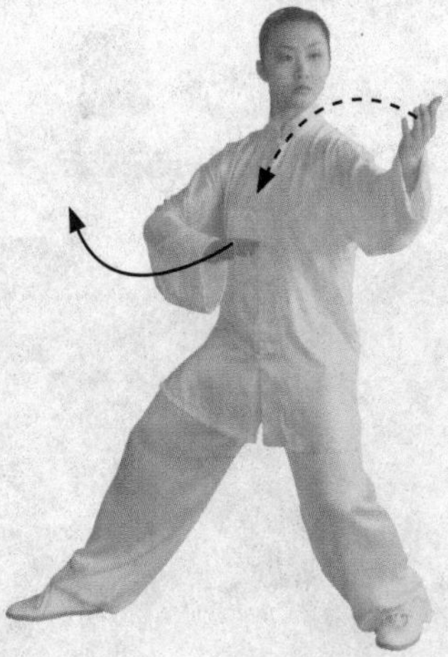

图73

4. 上体右转，左臂屈肘，
   双手相合，掌心相对，
   继续右转，双手向前，
   慢慢挤出，重心前移，
   成右弓步，看右手腕。
   （图74、图75）

图74

Turn torso slightly to right while bending left arm and touching the inside of right wrist with left palm. Torso keeps turning to left when pressing both hands forward, palms facing each other and continue to spin. Shift weight onto right leg for a right bow stance. Look at right wrist. (Fig 74, Fig 75)

图75

5. 两手分开，平抹下按，
   左腿屈膝，上体后坐，
   重心左移，右脚翘起，
   两手屈肘，收回腹前，
   双手手心，向前下方，
   目视前方。（图76～图78）

Turn both palms downward as left hand passes over right wrist and moves forward in a curve. Separate hands shoulder-width apart and draw them back to the front of abdomen, palms slightly downward. Then, sit back and shift weight onto left leg with knee bending, raise toe of right foot. Look forward. (Fig 76 - Fig 78)

图76

图77

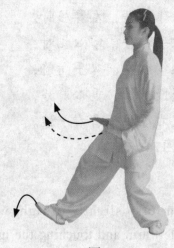

图78

图79

6. 上式不停，重心前移，
   两手按出，掌心向前，
   右腿前弓，成右弓步，
   目视前方。（图79）

Shift weight onto right leg while pushing palms upward, forward curve until hands at shoulder level. At the same time, bend right leg to make right bow stance. Look at forward. (Fig 79)

【 呼吸配合 】
[Breathing Method]

此式呼吸方法与"图53～图65"相同，唯左右方向相反。

The same with Fig 53 - Fig 65, only that the direction is opposition.

九、单鞭
Dan Bian

1. 上体后坐，重心左移，
　　右脚里扣，上体左转，
　　两手向左，弧形运转，
　　眼看左手。（图80、图81）

Sit back and shift weight onto left leg, turn right toe inward. While turning body to left, both hands move to left, with left hand above, until left arm is extended sideways at shoulder level, palm outward, and right hand is in front of left ribs, palm obliquely inward. Look at left hand. (Fig 80, Fig 81)

2. 重心右移，上体右转，
　　左脚点地，右手变勾，
　　左手向下，经由腹前，
　　右上划弧，至右肩前，
　　手心向里，眼看左手。
　　（图82、图83）

Turn body to right, shift weight onto right leg and draw left foot to the inner side of right foot, with toe touching ground. At the same time, right hand makes an arc upward and around to right until arm is at shoulder level. With right palm now turning outward and forming a hooked hand, left hand moves in a curve passing abdomen up to the front of right shoulder, palm inward. Look at left hand. (Fig 82, Fig 83)

图80

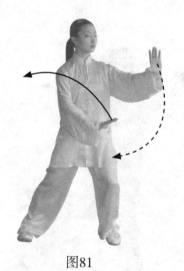

图81

图82

图83

3. 上体左转，左脚迈出，
右脚后蹬，成左弓步，
重心左移，跟随上体，
左掌翻转，向前推出，
手心向前，手眼齐平，
双臂微屈，眼看左手。
（图84、图85）

Turn body to left, left foot takes a step to left to make left bow stance. Shift weight onto left leg, turn left palm outward and push it forward with arm bending and fingertips at eyes level. (Fig 84, Fig 85)

图84

【 呼吸配合 】
[Breathing Method]

右手勾手时先吸后呼；左手向左推掌时，先吸后呼。这种动作一般需要两个呼吸周期，特别是最后的呼气要配合沉肩、松腹、沉胯同时完成。
（图81～图85）

There are two breathing periods in this series. Inhale first and then exhale when making right hand hook. Inhale first and then exhale when pushing left palm to the left. Especially the last exhalation must be cooperated with relaxing shoulders, waist and hips. (Fig 80 - Fig 85)

图85

十、云手
Wave Hands

图86

1. 重心右移，上体右转，
   右勾变掌，左手划弧，
   靠近右掌，目视右方。
   （图86～图88）

Sit back and shift weight onto right leg, turn body to right, with left toe turning inward. Meanwhile, move left hand in a curve passing abdomen to the front of right shoulder, palm obliquely inward; while right hand becomes palm, facing outward. Look at left hand. (Fig 86 - Fig 88)

图87

2. 重心左移，上体左转，
   两手划弧，向左云手，
   左脚跟步，两腿微屈，
   目视左方。（图89、图90）

Shift weight onto left leg and turn body to left. At the same rime, left hand moves in a curve passing face to left with palm turning slowly leftward, while right hand moves in a curve passing abdomen up to the front of left shoulder with palm slowly turning obliquely inward. As right hand moves upward, draw right foot to the inner side of left foot, feet paralleled. Look at left hand. (Fig 89, Fig 90)

图88

图89

图90

图91

图92

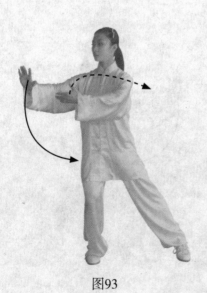

图93

3. 上体右转，左脚开步，
两手划弧，向右云手，
目视右方。（图91～图93）

Turn body to right, take a step to left,
circle with arms, wave hands to left. Look
at right. (Fig 91 - Fig 93)

4. 重心左移，上体左转，
   两手划弧，向左云手，
   左脚跟步，两腿微屈，
   目视左方。（图94、图95）

图94

Shift weight onto left leg and turn body to left. At the same rime, left hand moves in a curve passing face to left with palm turning slowly leftward, while right hand moves in a curve passing abdomen up to the front of left shoulder with palm slowly turning obliquely inward. As right hand moves upward, draw right foot to the inner side of left foot, feet paralleled. Look at left hand. (Fig 94, Fig 95)

图95

5. 上体右转，左脚开步，
   两手划弧，向右云手，
   目视右方。（图96～图98）

Turn body to right, take a step to left, circle with arms, wave hands to left. Look at right. (Fig 96 - Fig 98)

图96

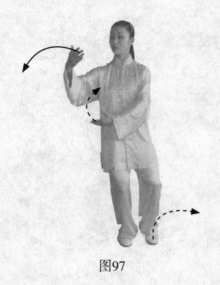

图97

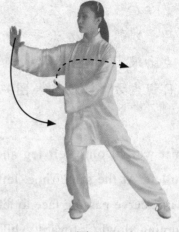

图98

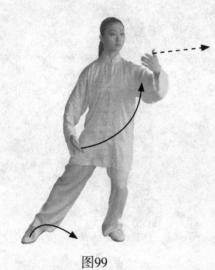

图99

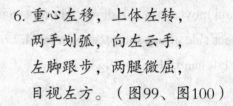

6. 重心左移，上体左转，
两手划弧，向左云手，
左脚跟步，两腿微屈，
目视左方。（图99、图100）

Shift weight onto left leg and turn
body to left. At the same rime, left hand
moves in a curve passing face to left with
palm turning slowly leftward, while right
hand moves in a curvc passing abdomen
up to the front of left shoulder with palm
slowly turning obliquely inward. As right
hand moves upward, draw right foot to the
inner side of left foot, feet paralleled. Look
at left hand. (Fig 99, Fig 100)

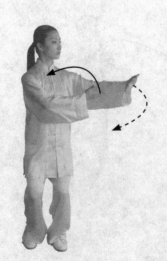

图100

【呼吸配合】
[Breathing Method]

向右云手时吸气，向左云手时呼气；同时步法要求左脚迈步时吸气，两脚并步时呼气。上下相随，呼吸搭配节奏均匀。（图86～图100）

Inhale when waving right hand to the right, and exhale when waving left hand to the left. Inhale when stepping left foot sideways to the left, and exhale when bring right foot to the inner side of left foot. Left hand is cooperated with right foot and right hand is cooperated with left foot. (Fig 86 - Fig 100)

图101

 十一、单鞭
Dan Bian

1. 上体右转，右手变勾，
   左手划弧，至右肩前，
   手心向内，重心下沉，
   落于右腿，左脚点地，
   眼看右手。（图101～图103）

图102

Turn torso to right, move right hand to right to make a hook hand while left band moves in a curve passing abdomen to front of right shoulder with palm turning inward. Shift weight onto the right leg, with left toe touching ground. Look at right hand. (Fig 101 - Fig 103)

图103

2. 上体左转，左脚左迈，

成左弓步，重心左移，

上体左转，左掌翻转，

向前推出，成"单鞭"式。

（图104、图105）

Turn body to left, take a step with left foot, then become a left bow step, shift weight on left, turn body to left and circle out with your left and palm, push forward, form "Dan Bian". (Fig 104, Fig 105)

图104

〖 呼吸配合 〗
[Breathing Method]

右手勾手时先吸后呼；左手向左推掌时，先吸后呼。这种动作一般需要两个呼吸周期，特别是最后的呼气要配合沉肩、松腹、沉胯同时完成。（图101～图105）

There are two breathing periods in this series. Inhale first and then exhale when making right hand hook. Inhale first and then exhale when pushing left palm to the left. Especially the last exhalation must be cooperated with relaxing shoulders, waist and hips. (Fig 101 - Fig 105)

图105

十二、高探马
Pat High on the Horse

1. 右脚向前，跟进半步，

重心后移，右手变掌，

两手翻转，手心向上，
两肘微屈，目视右手。
（图106）

Draw right foot half a step forward
and shift weight onto right leg. Open
right hand and turn both palms up, elbows
slightly bend, while body turns slightly
to right, lift left heel to make left empty
stance. Look at right hand. (Fig 106)

图106

2. 上体左转，右掌前推，
手心向前，手眼同高，
左手收回，左脚前移，
脚尖点地，成左虚步，
目视右手。（图107）

Turn body slightly to left, push right
palm forward passing right ear, fingertips
at eye level, while left hand moves to front
of abdomen, palm up. At the same time,
move left foot a bit forward, toe touching
ground. Look at right hand. (Fig 107)

【 呼吸配合 】
[Breathing Method]

右脚跟半步，两手托掌时吸气；左
脚前点地、右掌前推时呼气。（图106、
图107）

图107

Inhale when bring right foot forward in
half step, and exhale when left toe touches
ground and push right palm forward.
(Fig 106, Fig 107)

图108

1. 左手前伸，两手交叉，
   向下划弧，左脚提起，
   向前垫步，重心前移，
   右腿蹬直，成左弓步，
   目视前方。（图108～图110）

Turn torso slightly to right and cross hands by extending left hand, palm up onto back of right wrist. Then separate hands, moving both in a downward curve with palms turning downward. Meanwhile, left foot takes a step to left front to make left bow stance, toe turns slightly outward. Look at forward. (Fig 108 - Fig 110)

图109

2. 双手划弧，抱于胸前，
   右手在外，手心向内，
   右脚收提，脚尖点地，
   看右前方。（图111）

Both hands keep moving in a downward, inward, upward curve until wrists cross in front of chest, with right hand in front and both palms turn inward. Meanwhile, draw right foot to the inner side of left foot, with toe touching ground. Look at right. (Fig 111)

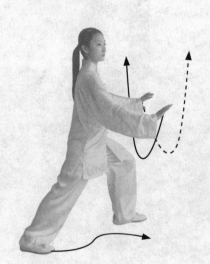

图110

3. 双臂划弧，分开平举，
   肘部微屈，手心向外，
   右腿屈膝，随即提起，
   右脚蹬出，眼看右手。
   （图112、图113）

图111

Push hands out sideways at shoulder level with elbows slightly bending and palms turn outward. Meanwhile, lift right knee and thrust foot slowly forward. Look at right hand. (Fig 112, Fig 113)

【 呼吸配合 】

[Breathing Method]

两手向上分掌时吸气，两手收抱胸前时呼气，右腿提膝时吸气，蹬脚时呼气，同时两手向外撑开。
（图108～图113）

图112

Inhale when separating both hands sideways; exhale when crossing hands in front of the chest. Inhale when lifting right knee; exhale when straightening right leg. (Fig 108 - Fig 113)

图113

图114

十四、双峰贯耳
Strike Opponent's Ears with Both Fists

1. 右腿收回，随后屈膝，
  两手翻转，手心向上，
  向下划弧，落右膝侧，
  目视前方。（图114、图115）

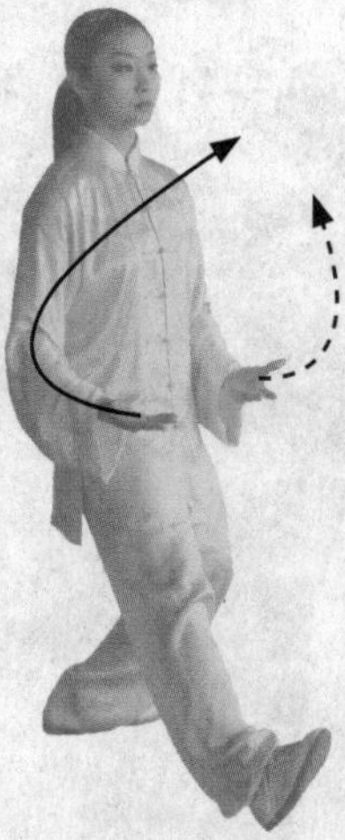

Bend right leg at knee. Meanwhile, Turn both palms up, dropping to the side of right knee. Look at forward. (Fig 114, Fig 115)

图115

2. 右脚落下，重心前移，
  成右弓步，两掌变拳，
  经由两侧，向前贯打，
  两拳相对，高与耳齐，
  拳眼向下，眼看右拳。
  （图116、图117）

Drop right foot on ground to right front, shifting weight onto right leg to make a right bow stance. At the same time, lower hands to both sides and gradually clench fists; then move them backward with arms turning inward, keep moving them upward and forward for a pincer movement that ends at eyes level with fists 10-20 cm apart, fists holes facing diagonally downward. Look at right fist. (Fig 116, Fig 117)

图116

【呼吸配合】
[Breathing Method]

接上一动作，右腿屈膝收回时吸气，然后向前迈步落地时呼气，两拳向上提时吸气，向中间合拢"贯耳"时呼气。（图114～图117）

Inhale when bending right knee; exhale when landing right foot to ground.

Inhale when raising both arms upward, and exhale when closing up both fists in front of the face. (Fig 114 - Fig 117)

图117

十五、转身左蹬脚
Kick with Left Leg

1. 左腿屈膝，随即后坐，
重心左移，上体左转，
右脚里扣，两拳变掌，
划弧平举，手心向前，
目视左手。（图118、图119）

图118

Shift weight onto left leg, turn body to left with right toe turning inward. Meanwhile, open both fists and separate hands in an upward curve, extending both arms sideways, with palms facing forward. Look at left hand. (Fig 118, Fig 119)

图119

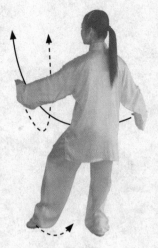

图120

2. 重心左移，左脚内收，
   脚尖点地，双手划弧，
   抱于胸前，左手在外，
   手心向内，目视左方。
   （图120、图121）

Shift weight onto right leg and draw left foot to the inner side of right foot, with toe touching ground. At the same time, cross hands in front of chest, with palms facing inward. Look at left. (Fig 120, Fig 121)

图121

3. 两臂划弧，分开平举，
   肘部微屈，手心向外，
   左腿屈膝，随即提起，
   左脚蹬出，目视左手。
   （图122、图123）

Separate hands sideways at shoulders level, with elbows slightly bending and palms facing outward. Meanwhile, lift left knee and kick foot forward on left. Look at left hand. (Fig 122, Fig 123)

图122

图123

【 呼吸配合 】

[Breathing Method]

两手向上分掌时吸气，两手收
抱胸前时呼气，左腿提膝时吸气，
蹬脚时呼气，同时两掌向外撑开。
（图118～图123 ）

Inhale when separating both hands
sideways; exhale when crossing hands in
front of the chest. Inhale when lifting left
knee; exhale when straightening left leg.
(Fig 118 - Fig 123)

图124

十六、左下势独立
Push Down and Stand on Left Leg

1. 左腿收回，上体右转，
   右掌变勾，左掌划弧，
   至右肩前，掌心斜后，
   目视右手。（图124、图125 ）

Pull back left foot with knee bending.
Turn torso to right. Make right hand hook
while moving left hand in a curve passing
face to the front of right shoulder, palm
turning inward. Look at right hand.
(Fig 124, Fig 125)

图125

2. 右腿下蹲，左腿伸出，
   成左仆步，左手下落，
   向前穿出，目视左手。
   （图126、图127 ）

图126

图127

Turn torso to left, and crouch down on right leg, stretch left leg sideways on left, move left hand down to left along the inner side of left leg, palm turning outward. Look at left hand. (Fig 126, Fig 127)

3. 重心前移，左腿前弓，
   左手前穿，右手勾手，
   置于身后。（图128）

Straighten right leg and shift weight onto left leg with left knee bending. At the same time, keep moving left hand to front with palm facing right, while right hand drops behind the back, with bunching fingertips pointing upward. Look at left hand. (Fig 128)

图128

4. 左腿独立，右膝上提，
   右臂曲肘，举于胸前，
   掌尖向上，左手下落，
   置于胯旁。（图129、图130）

Lift right knee slowly as right hand opens into a palm and swings to front passing outside of right leg, with elbow bending. Move left hand down to the side of left hip, with palm down. Look at right hand. (Fig 129, Fig130)

图129

【 呼吸配合 】
[Breathing Method]

下势仆步时呼气，左掌向上穿时吸气，身体起立弓步时呼气，接着，右掌上提时吸气，独立站稳后呼气，同时配合右肘下沉。（图124～图130）

Exhale when making crouch stance. Inhale when moving left palm forward along left leg with fingers pointing forward. Exhale when making left bow stance and then inhale when raising right palm upward. Exhale when standing on left leg with right elbow dropping. (Fig 124 - Fig 130)

图130

十七、右下势独立
Push Down and Stand on Right Leg

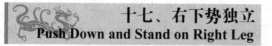

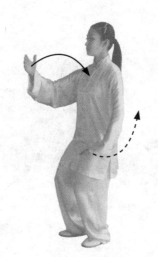

图131

1. 右脚下落，身体左转，
左手后举，变成勾手，
右掌划弧，至左肩前，
掌心斜后，目视左手。
（图131、图132）

Put right foot down in front of left foot, with toe touching ground. Turn body to left. At the same time, lift left hand sideways to shoulders level and make it hook while right hand moves in a curve to front of left shoulder with fingers pointing up. Look at left hand. (Fig 131, Fig 132)

图132

图133

2. 左腿下蹲，右腿伸出，
　　成右仆步，右手下落，
　　向前穿出，眼看右手。
　　（图133、图134）

Turn torso to right, and crouch down on left leg, stretch right leg sideways on right. Move right hand down and to right along the inner side of right leg, palm turning outward. Look at right hand. (Fig 133, Fig 134)

3. 重心前移，右腿前弓，
　　右手前穿，左手勾手，
　　置于身后。（图135）

Straighten left leg and shift weight onto right leg with right knee bending. At the same time, keep moving right hand to front with palm facing left, while left hand drops behind the back, with bunching fingertips pointing upward. Look at right hand. (Fig 135)

图134

4. 右腿独立，左膝上提，
　　左臂屈肘，举于胸前，
　　掌尖向上，右手下落，
　　置于胯旁。（图136、图137）

Lift left knee slowly as left hand opens into a palm and swings to front passing outside of left leg, with elbow bending. Move right hand down to the side of right hip, with palm down. Look at left hand. (Fig 136, Fig 137)

图135

【呼吸配合】

[Breathing Method]

下势仆步时呼气，右掌向上穿时吸气，身体起立弓步时呼气，接着左掌上提时吸气，独立站稳后呼气，同时配合左肘下沉。（图131～图137）

Exhale when making crouch stance. Inhale when moving right palm forward along right leg with fingers pointing forward. Exhale when making right bow stance and then inhale when raising left palm upward. Exhale when standing on right leg with left elbow dropping. (Fig 131 - Fig 137)

图136

图137

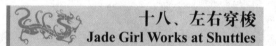
十八、左右穿梭
Jade Girl Works at Shuttles

1. 身体左转，左脚落地，
   脚尖外撇，双手相对，
   成抱球状，右脚内收，
   至左脚侧，脚尖点地，
   看左前臂。（图138～图140）

Turn body to left and put left foot on floor in front of right foot, with toe turning outward. At the same time, make a hold-ball gesture in front of left part of chest, with left hand on top. Then move the right foot to the inner side of left foot, with toe touching ground. Look at left forearm. (Fig 138 - Fig 140)

图138

图139

图140

图141

图142

图143

2. 身体右转，右脚迈出，
成右弓步，右手上举，
手心斜上，左手立掌，
向前推出，高与鼻平，
手心向前，目视左手。
（图141～图143）

Turn body to right while right foot
takes a step forward to right to make right
bow stance. At the same time, move right
hand up to right front, and palm turns
obliquely upward, while left palm pushes
out forward and upward to nose level,
Look at left hand. (Fig 141 - Fig 143)

3. 右脚外撇，重心右移，
左脚跟进，脚尖点地，
两手相对，成抱球状，
看右前臂。（图144、图145）

Turn body slightly to right, shifting weight backward, with right toe turned outward. Then shift weight back onto right leg and draw left foot to the inner side of right foot, with toe touching on ground. Meanwhile, make a hold-ball gesture in front of right chest, with right hand on top. Look at right forearm. (Fig 144, Fig 145)

图144

4. 身体左转，左脚迈出，
成左弓步，左手上举，
手心斜上，右手立掌，
向前推出，高与鼻平，
手心向前，眼看右手。
（图146～图148）

Turn body to left while left foot takes a step forward to left to make left bow stance. At the same time, move left hand up to left front, and palm turns obliquely upward, while right palm pushes out forward and upward to nose level, Look at right hand. (Fig 146 - Fig 148)

图145

【 呼吸配合 】
[Breathing Method]

左穿梭：右手上架时吸气，左手前推时呼气。右穿梭：左手上架时吸气，右手前推时呼气。（图138～图148）

图146

Left style: inhale when blocking upward with night arm; exhale when pushing left palm forward. Right style: same as left style, reversing "right" and "left". (Fig 138 - Fig 148)

图147

十九、海底针
Needle at the Bottom of the Sea

右脚向前，跟进半步，
左脚前移，脚尖点地，
成左虚步，右手上提，
由右耳旁，斜前下插，
指尖斜下，与此同时，
左手划弧，落左胯旁，
手心向下，指尖向前，
看前下方。（图149、图150）

图148

Right foot takes a half step forward, shift weight onto right leg and move left foot a bit forward to make left empty stance. At the same time, body turns slightly to right and then to left, right hand moves down in front of body, up to the side of right ear and then obliquely downward in front of the body, with the palm facing left and fingers pointing obliquely downward, while left hand moves in a forward, downward curve to the side of left hip, with palm down. Look at forward. (Fig 149, Fig 150)

图149

【 呼吸配合 】

[Breathing Method]

接上一动作，右脚跟半步，右掌上提时吸气；接着左脚尖前点地，右掌下探时呼气。（图149、图150）

Inhale when bring right foot forward in half step and raising right palm upward; exhale when touching ground with left toe and moving right palm downward. (Fig 149, Fig 150)

图150

二十、闪通臂
Deflect with Arm

上体右转，左脚前迈，
屈膝弓腿，成左弓步，
右手上提，屈臂上举，
于右额上，左手前推，
高与鼻平，手心向前，
目视左手。（图151～图153）

图151

Turn body slightly to right and take a step forward with left foot to make a left bow stance. At the same time, lift right hand with elbow bending to stop in front of right temple, arm turns inward with thumb pointing down, while left palm pushes forward at nose level. Look at left hand. (Fig 151 - Fig 153)

图152

图153

[Breathing Method]

右掌上架时吸气，左掌顺步前推时呼气。（图151～图153）

Inhale when blocking upward with right arm, exhale when pushing left palm forward. (Fig 151 - Fig 153)

二十一、转身搬拦捶
Turn Body with Parry and Punch

图154

1. 上体后坐，重心右移，
   左脚内扣，转向右后，
   与此同时，右手变拳，
   至左肋旁，拳心向下，
   左掌上举，置于头前，
   掌心斜上，目视前方。
   （图154、图155、图155附）

Sit back and shift weight onto right leg. Turn body to right with left toe turned inward. Then shift weight back onto left leg. Following the body turning, move right hand in a rightward, downward curve with fingers clenching into fist, passing abdomen to the side of left ribs, while left hand moves up to the front of forehead, with palm obliquely up. Look at forward. (Fig 154, Fig 155, Fig 155App)

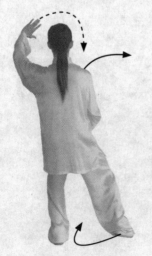

图155

2. 右拳翻转，向前搬出，
　　拳心向上，左手下落，
　　于左胯旁，掌心向下，
　　右脚收回，随即前迈，
　　脚尖外撇，目视右拳。
（图156、图156附、图157）

Turn body to right, moving right fist
up and then forward and downward for a
backhand pound, meanwhile lower left
hand to the side of left hip with palm
down. At the same time, right foot draws
to left foot and takes a step forward, with
toe turning outward. Look at right fist.
(Fig 156, Fig 156App, Fig 157)

图155附

图156

图156附

图157

图158

3. 重心右移，左脚上步，
　左手上提，划弧拦出，
　右拳划弧，收至右腰，
　拳心向上，目视左手。
　（图158、图159）

Shift weight onto right leg and take
a step forward with left foot. Meanwhile,
move left hand sideways and up to front to
parry, palm turns slightly downward while
withdraw right fist in a curve to the side of
right waist. Look at left hand.
(Fig 158, Fig 159)

4. 左腿前弓，成左弓步，
　右手冲拳，拳眼向上，
　高与胸平，目视右拳。
　（图160）

图159

Bend left leg to make a left bow
stance, strike out right fist forward at chest
level, while left hand withdraws to the side
of right forearm. Look at right fist. (Fig
160)

【 呼吸配合 】
[Breathing Method]

　转身时随着身体重心移动，先
吸后呼；"搬"捶时右拳上提吸气，
向前"搬"打时呼气，然后，左手
"拦"时吸气，接着右拳冲出时呼气。
（图154～图160）

图160

Inhale first and then exhale when turning body and shifting body weight onto right leg. Inhale when raising right fist upward; exhale when pounding with right fist. Inhale when parrying with left palm; exhale when punching with right fist. (Fig 154 - Fig 160)

图161

二十二、如封似闭
Apparent Close-up

1. 右拳变掌，两掌上翻，
　随后分开，身体后坐，
　左脚翘起，重心右移，
　目视前方。（图161~图163）

图162

Left hand stretches forward from below right wrist. Cross two hands with palms up. Separate hands and pull them back, while shifting weight onto right leg, with left toe lifting. Look at forward. (Fig 161 - Fig 163)

图163

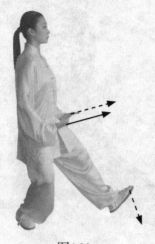

图164

2. 手置胸前，双手翻掌，
经由腹前，向前推出，
腕与肩平，手心向前，
左腿前弓，成左弓步，
目视前方。（图164～图166）

Turn palms down in front of chest, push them downward passing abdomen and then forward and upward until wrists are at shoulders level, with palms facing forward. At the same time, bend left knee to make a left bow stance. Look at forward. (Fig 164 - Fig 166)

图165

〖 呼吸配合 〗
[Breathing Method]

身体重心后移，两掌收回时吸气，两掌向前推时呼气。（图161～图166）

Inhale when moving body weight backward and pulling both hands in, exhale when push both palms forward. (Fig 161 -Fig 166)

二十三、十字手
Cross Hands

1. 屈膝后坐，重心右移，
左脚里扣，向右转体，
跟随转体，右手划弧，
掌心向前，肘部微屈，
上体右转，右脚外撇，

图166

成右弓步，目视右手。

（图167、图168）

Sit back and shift weight onto right leg with right knee bending. Turn body to right with left toe turning inward. Following body turning, move both bands sideways in a horizontal curve at shoulders level, palms forward and elbows slightly bend. Meanwhile, turn right toe outward and shift weight onto right leg. Look at right hand. (Fig 167, Fig 168)

图167

2. 重心左移，右脚回收，
   与肩同宽，两腿蹬直，
   成开立步，两手向下，
   经过腹前，向上划弧，
   交叉合抱，置于胸前，
   两臂撑圆，腕与肩平，
   右手在外，成十字手，
   手心向后，眼看前方。

（图169、图170）

图168

Shift weight onto left leg with right toe turned inward. Then move right foot towards left foot to make them parallel to each other and shoulder-width apart; straighten legs gradually. At the same time, move both hands down in a vertical curve and cross them in front of abdomen, then raise the crossed hands to chest level with wrists at shoulders level, right palm on the outside and palms facing inward. Look at forward. (Fig 169, Fig170)

图169

图170

[Breathing Method]

身体右转，两手向外分掌时吸气，向下抱时呼气，双手胸前交叉时吸气。（图167～图170）

Inhale when turning body to the right and separating palms to both sides. Exhale when lowering both hands, inhale when crossing hands in front of the chest. (Fig 167 - Fig 170)

图171

二十四、收式
The Closing Form

两掌外翻，手心向下，
两臂下落，停于体侧，
左腿靠拢，并步直立，
目视前方。（图171～图173）

Turn palms forward and downward at shoulders level while lowering both hands gradually to the side of hips. Look at forward. (Fig 171 - Fig 173)

【呼吸配合】

[Breathing Method]

上动不停，两手前伸时呼气，身体站起时吸气，两手放下时呼气。两脚并步时吸气，站定后呼气。（图171～图173）

图172

Keep moving upper body, exhale when extending both arms forward. Inhale when straightening both knees; exhale when lowering both palms; inhale when bringing left foot to right foot, and then exhale. (Fig 171 - Fig 173)

图173